FROM WATER TO WINE

REVEALING GOD'S GLORY IN THE FACE OF ADVERSITY

ELORM MENSA

FROM WATER TO WINE

REVEALING GOD'S GLORY IN THE FACE OF ADVERSITY

ELORM MENSA

Published by

EMMI Publishing

P.O. Box AF 345

Adenta, Ghana

Cover design by Apex Vision Grafix, Accra, Ghana.

Elorm Mensa Ministries International

Accra, Ghana

www.elormmensa.com

Table of Contents

Dedication

To people all over the world who are struggling to believe in their uniqueness and strength because of the situations surrounding them.

To people who have suffered tremendous loss and pain, so much that they do not have strength to hope again.

To people who feel insignificant and dwarfed by a world system that does not yet recognize their gift.

I was inspired to write this book to usher you into a new season of extraordinary possibilities and miracles. May you be strengthened to rise above the circumstances keeping you down, to reveal the greatness within you.

The world awaits your manifestation.

FOREWORD

The Lord God clearly discloses to us in the scriptures that, He knows the plans and the thoughts He has for us. They are plans that are designed to bring us to an expected end. It is important to appreciate this truth; that the end is glory and nothing less than that. The path of the righteous man is as a shining light, that shines brighter and brighter to a perfect day. By the revelation of scriptures, the end of the saint is Christ. That is the glory of the saint.

Now, the saint can only come into that glory by walking in the light of the perspective of Christ. The psalmist said, *"In thine light we shall see light."* (Psalm 36:9) The saint is called to walk in the light of the risen Christ, see and do things the way Christ Jesus would.

Jesus Christ in his earthly sojourn never called events that seemed negative as they presented themselves; He had a different viewpoint to them. He always saw the glory of God concealed in the stories of men. He always saw advantages concealed in adversity. He always saw the negatives having the positives. He saw darkness working for light. He saw adversities as the canvas on which the most beautiful thoughts of God are painted into reality for all to stand in awe viewing them.

Adversities are not evil, but they are opportunities to unveil glory, beauty and the splendour of the Lord. As a Christian it is expected of you to see as your Father in heaven sees. God does not see adversities, He sees glory.

In this beautifully written material, the author with the help of The Holy Spirit, tries to unveil in every page the agenda of God hidden in every adversity that characterises our existence, and how the reader can be rightly positioned to fully maximise the advantages that adversities present.

Dear reader, I assure you that you are about to mingle with great wisdom. In every word in this material is the wisdom for a victorious living, skilfully crafted. This is not just another information book, but a transformation agent. The contents of this book are beyond mere motivation, but activation of truth for desired outcome in the face of adversity.

I can boldly say to you dear reader, that what the enemy

sought to achieve with a misconception of adversity, by understanding, will become the vitamins for your advantage and advancement.

The Lord bless you as you delve into this ocean of great treasures.

Great Grace!

Isaiah Fosu-Kwakye Jnr.
(Pastor, Music Minister and Author)

Introduction

In the small town of Cana in Galilee, it was a time of joy and celebration; family and friends joined the bride and bridegroom in a feast in honour of their marriage. Such celebrations were a customary part of Jewish weddings, and guests came with the full assurance that they will be well catered for. There was music, and laughter, and feasting. By all indications, it was going to be a beautiful day.

However, amidst the merriment and fanfare, trouble was brewing. Mary looked on in dismay as the wine ran out ahead of schedule. All of a sudden, what started out as a day of joy was about to become a day of shame. How could you have a feast without wine? Knowing very well the implications and disgrace associated with running out of wine at a wedding feast, Mary turns to the one person she knows can avert this disaster. She goes to Jesus, who was at the wedding with his disciples, and says, "They have no wine." Jesus replied, "That is not our problem. My time has not yet come."

It is interesting to note that, though Mary does not get an encouraging response from Jesus, she is so convinced that something good was about to happen. So strong is her conviction, she turns to the servants and tells them, "Do whatever he tells you." The servants now look expectantly at Jesus waiting to respond to "whatever he tells you". He turns to them and instructs them to fill the six purification jars with water. I daresay none of the servants could have predicted that instruction. However, they obey and fill the jars to the brim.

Well, if they thought the first instruction was strange, they were in for a bigger surprise. He tells them, "Draw some out, and take it to the governor of the feast." Though confused, they obey and serve the governor out of the water they fetched. The governor tastes it and his face lights up. He calls out to the bridegroom and says, ""Every man serves the good wine first; and when men have drunk freely, then the poor wine; but you have kept the good wine until now." In essence, the governor was saying, this wine is superior to what we have had so far.

The bridegroom has no clue what he is talking about; but the servants knew, Mary knew, and the disciples of Jesus knew. There, in the small town of Cana in Galilee, the Son of God had just demonstrated his glory by turning water into wine to avert a crisis.

"This beginning of signs Jesus did in Cana of Galilee, and manifested His glory; and His disciples believed in Him." *– John 2:11*

In His first public manifestation of His glory, Jesus opens to us an eternal truth that is more significant than just rescuing a wedding feast from collapse. Jesus, The Word, makes a statement: I reveal my glory by turning what is ordinary into something extraordinary; by converting the neglected and making them celebrated; by transforming seasons of adversity into seasons of prosperity.

All through scripture, God consistently shows His ability to glorify Himself through things, people or situations that have no glory. Whether it be changing a childless Abraham to become a father of many nations, turning a shepherd boy into Israel's greatest king, defeating a world superpower, Egypt, with a rod-wielding Moses, converting a harlot to become a virtuous lady of Israel, bringing a dead and stinking Lazarus back to life; and we can go on and on. It is not God's nature to just sympathise with the afflicted, or endorse the sorrows of His people; His nature is to show up and show-off.

The purpose of this book is to bring an understanding of God's workings in our lives, and show you how to position yourself in order to turn your trials into triumphs. As you go through this book, may God make you an undeniable proof of His glory and power. Amen.

CHAPTER ONE

Adversity is a Certainty

Every success story has a chapter of adversity.

Everyone on earth, at one point or another has gone, is going, or will go through a period of adversity. Problems are not strange to humanity. No matter our differences, irrespective of our race, religion, social status or academic qualifications, we all have periods of adversity. Kings have problems, servants have problems; rich people have problems, so do the poor; Africans, Europeans, Asians; all face difficulties in this journey of life.

Success stories of great men and women are laden with moments of hardship and toil; perseverance in the face of great opposition. No matter how well we plan, or how careful we try to be, we are bound to encounter a few difficult and uncomfortable bumps on our road to success. Nelson Mandela will forever be remembered as a global icon of peace and one of Africa's most celebrated heroes, but his incredible story has a 27-year chapter that was spent in prison. Benjamin Franklin had to drop out of school at age 10, but today he is recognized as one of the founding fathers of America, and has his image on the $100 bill. Apostle Paul was threatened with death, beaten, imprisoned, but is still regarded as one of the greatest apostles of Christ. Job was one of the richest men in his time, but at a point in his life, he lost all his wealth, all his children and was struck with a terrible disease. The list is endless.

Unfortunately, many people have faced similar situations and used it as an excuse to remain down in life. Dreams have been abandoned, companies have folded up, and great destinies have ended up in obscurity because people could not find a way out of their season of adversity. They chose rather to blame others, society, and anything that can be blamed in their quest to justify their failure.

Man was created to handle adversity.

There is no genuine excuse for failure. God created man and put in us the innate ability to handle every negative situation that life throws at us.

"Then God blessed them, and God said to them, 'Be fruitful and multiply; fill the earth and SUBDUE IT; HAVE DOMINION over the fish of the sea, over the birds of the air, and over every living thing that moves on the earth.'" – Genesis 1:28 (emphasis added)

When God was giving man his mandate of operation, He told man to be fruitful and multiply, and also added one important element – **SUBDUE IT.** The word "subdue" means to conquer and bring into subjection. It means to bring under control especially by an exertion of the will. God then goes ahead to say, **HAVE DOMINION**, which is translated from the Hebrew word, *Rādāh*, which means to prevail against or to subjugate. In essence, God was telling man, you are the boss, so act like it. There will be issues that will challenge your authority, but you must bring them under control. God knew that man would face problems on earth, and so He equipped us to adequately handle them. There would be no need for dominion if there was no opposition or likelihood of chaos and rebellion.

It is interesting to note that the first chapter of the Bible, Genesis 1, tells us how God encountered adversity on earth. The first verse of that chapter says, *"In the beginning, God created the heaven and the earth."* Now God the Creator comes to see His creation in verse 2, and alas, it is without form, it is void, and it is full of darkness. If you were not convinced that adversity is inevitable on earth, this should bring it home for you. God Himself had to address a negative situation on earth. The first glimpse the Bible gives us of our Heavenly Father, is one who turns a formless and dark entity called earth and makes it a wonder and a beauty.

By the 26th verse of that same chapter, God says, ***"Let us make man in our image, after our likeness."*** God says, let us create mankind to behave just like us; people who will encounter darkness and call forth light, who will meet emptiness and bring forth abundance, people who can create something beautiful out of something formless. It is no wonder why God will charge man to **SUBDUE AND HAVE DOMINION!** God does not expect you to be a victim of your environment; that does not depict dominion. God did not create you to give excuses or to accept defeat. You are meant to transform every negative situation and bring forth a testimony.

You are not the first person to encounter problems and you will not be the last; so do not ever feel like you are at a disadvantage or you are cursed just because you are facing opposition. It is an inevitable part of our life on earth. You are designed by your Heavenly Father to handle whatever comes your way.

God promised victory not leisure.

God has never promised an opposition-free life. Everyone He called and used had to face adversity one way or another.

What He promises is victory in spite of the opposition.

The promised land He had for Israel was not an amusement park where they just stroll in and have fun. It was a land occupied by countries who had great armies, tall walls, giants and mountains. They had to fight the Canaanites, Hittites, Amorites, Perizzites, Hivites and Jebusites for the promised land. They had to find a way past an overflowing River Jordan and the thick impregnable walls of Jericho. It was not a smooth journey, however, God's word came to pass; they inhabited the promised land. The surety of the promise did not insulate them from adversity but it guaranteed their triumph.

Jesus promised the disciples that they were going to demonstrate His power on earth by performing great signs and wonders; but he also prepared them for opposition by telling them:

"And you will be hated by all for My name's sake. But he who endures to the end will be saved." – Matthew 10:22

"These things I have spoken to you, that in Me you may have peace. In the world you will have tribulation; but be of good cheer, I have overcome the world." – John 16:33

Be of good cheer, because your victory is guaranteed. God is not a man to lie. Every promise of God will be fulfilled no matter the opposition. He has so designed it, that no matter what happens, the final chapter of the story is a chapter of victory.

CHAPTER TWO

THE PURPOSE OF ADVERSITY

The ultimate purpose of adversity is to reveal God's glory in you.

In order to fully understand the purpose of adversity, we must first understand the purpose of MANKIND. If we do not understand MAN we will not be able to comprehend the role adversity plays in his life. The working document that initiated the creation of man is summarized in Genesis 1:26.

"Then God said, 'Let Us make man in Our image, according to Our likeness; let them have dominion over the fish of the sea, over the birds of the air, and over the cattle, over all the earth and over every creeping thing that creeps on the earth.'"

Man was created to be God's representative on earth. Man is the centrepiece of creation, the one designed to be like the creator and keep all things in order. To an extent, all of creation reflects the glory of God. But with man, there is a difference. Man was given the nature of God and given the will to consciously display that nature when the need arises. Man is the creation that has been given the license to act like the Creator. Anytime man acts according to the original plan in Genesis 1:26, God is glorified.

"When I see and consider Your heavens, the work of your fingers, the moon and the stars which You have established, What is man that You are mindful of him, and the son of [earthborn] man that You care for him?

Yet You have made him a little lower than God, and You have crowned him with glory and honour.

You made him to have dominion over the works of your hands; You have put all things under his feet, all sheep and oxen, and also the beasts of the field,

The birds of the air, and the fish of the sea, whatever passes through the paths of the seas. O Lord, our Lord, how majestic and glorious and excellent is Your name in all the earth." – Psalm 8:3-9 (Amplified)

If the ultimate purpose of man is to reveal God's Glory, then it is imperative for him to be in an environment that motivates him to act accordingly. The glory of a teabag is seen not in a beautifully packaged box on a shelf, but rather in a cup of hot water. In that environment, the teabag glorifies its maker by releasing that which was hidden in it. The beauty and glory of gold is seen after it has been refined in the furnace under high temperatures.

The ultimate purpose of adversity is to bring out the divine nature that is hidden inside us. Every person on earth is a carrier of God's divine nature. Our existence finds meaning when we are able to express that which is embedded inside us. What adversity does is to compel us to let go of what is hidden inside. The problems you encounter are a clue to the potential you carry.

What will be your reaction if you put a teabag in a cup of hot water and instead of getting an infusion, the water remains the same and the teabag just shrinks in the water? You will obviously be upset and will want to have a word with the manufacturer because the product did not function as it was supposed to. The hot water was supposed to bring out the glory deposited in the teabag by the manufacturer, but the product did not positively respond to the environment created.

Anytime we give up in the face of adversity, we are malfunctioning and robbing God of the glory He deserves. The right response to every season of adversity is the manifestation of the divine nature locked up inside us.

Whenever there is a right response, God is glorified.

"Let your light so shine before men, that they may see your good works and glorify your Father in heaven." – Matthew 5:16

God creates adversity for His glory.

Moses was eighty years old when he encountered God on mount Horeb. He was a fugitive and he was a stammerer, and yet he was God's choice to deliver Israel from Egypt, the world's superpower at the time.

As Moses made his way with Aaron to Pharaoh's palace after encountering God through the burning bush that wasn't consumed, he must have been feeling very optimistic. He had just spoken to the God of Abraham, Isaac and Jacob, the One who is the **"I AM"**, and had also just seen some unbelievable miracles on Mount Horeb; Pharaoh would have no choice than to release the Israelites. However, Moses was in for a rude shock. What he did not envisage was Pharaoh increasing the burden of Israel after a "Thus saith the Lord." This was Pharaoh's response after Moses' well-rehearsed speech:

"Load them down with more work. Make them sweat! That will teach them to listen to lies." – Exodus 5:9 (NLT)

Instead of freeing his people, Moses had just made their lives more miserable. Instead of being a hero, he had just become the most annoying and most hated Hebrew. The Israelites did not hide their disappointment; they were better off before he came. In his frustration, Moses goes back to God with the one question almost every believer asks when in trouble: "Why? I did everything right, I obeyed your word and acted in faith. Why did it not work?"

It was then that God gave Moses a peek into the divine plan. Pharaoh needed to be stubborn in order for God to punish Egypt. The difficulty Moses encountered was actually a divine opportunity orchestrated from heaven. The ten mighty signs that God demonstrated in Egypt through Moses were necessary just because Pharaoh's heart was hardened. If Pharaoh had said yes after the first visit, how would the nations around hear of the wondrous acts of God and fear him?

"And I will harden Pharaoh's heart, and multiply My signs and My wonders in the land of Egypt.

But Pharaoh will not heed you, so that I may lay My hand on Egypt and bring My armies and My people, the children of Israel, out of the land of Egypt by great judgments.

And the Egyptians shall know that I am the LORD, when I stretch out My hand on Egypt and bring out the children of Israel from among them." – Exodus 7:3-5

By the time the tenth plague was over, everyone in Egypt was more than convinced that the God of Israel was greater than any other god. Even the nations around heard of it and shuddered. Moses was now revered and the Israelites were seen as a people to be feared. What a great feeling to experience such tremendous display of God's power! However, it all began by God hardening the heart of Pharaoh against Moses. God had to necessarily create an uncomfortable situation for Moses, in order to give him an enviable position of glory.

God's purpose for your life is not to make you comfortable, but rather make you a showpiece of His glory, which is why He has created the right environment of adversity that will squeeze out the glory in you. If you have been called by God for an assignment, no matter how big or small, rest assured that any opposition or affliction is just creating a conducive environment for a testimony. Apostle Paul put it beautifully in his second letter to the Church in Corinth.

"For our light affliction, which is but for a moment, is working for us a far more exceeding and eternal weight of glory." – 2Corinthians 4:17

It is the desire of your Heavenly Father, that every affliction will work out a far more exceeding and eternal weight of glory. It is not supposed to work out depression, doubt or anger. Paul was speaking from a point of personal experience, and he was trying to convey the same faith he had to the church. He made a comparison between the affliction and the glory; he called the affliction, light and temporary, and he described the glory as a far more exceeding and eternal weight.

In no other person is this truth more clearly illustrated than in the life of Jesus. He came with the noblest of missions, the purest of hearts and the backing of the Most High God. If anyone needed a comfortable and stress-free life on earth, it had to be Jesus. However, we see the Son of God endure abuse, affliction and crucifixion at the hands of those He created. It is only then, that the fullness of His glory is made manifest and He is given a name above every other name. The whole world will behold Him in His glory: every knee shall bow and every tongue will confess that Jesus is Lord! This glory was birthed not in a castle, but on a cross. After His resurrection, He appeared to some of the disciples and made a profound statement:

"Was it not necessary for the Christ to suffer these things and [only then to] enter His glory?" – Luke 24:26 (Amplified)

The cross was necessary, the stripes were necessary, the abuse and insults were all necessary, because they paved the way to eternal glory. That was God's plan, and it worked to perfection. What a joy to know that every season of adversity is actually a vehicle designed by God to transport you to your place of distinction. Affliction only comes to pave the way for the glory of God to be seen in you.

God permits adversity for His glory.

"The thief does not come except to steal, and to kill, and to destroy. I have come that they may have life, and that they may have it more abundantly." – John 10:10

There is an adversary of God's people, the devil, who has a 3-fold mandate according to John 10:10 – to steal, kill and destroy. After he was thrown out of heaven, his main occupation has been to resist the will of God on earth, and to prevent us from discovering and manifesting our divine nature. Whether he comes with subtle and appetising temptations, or he comes with a torrent of misfortune, persecution and trouble, the devil's aim remains the same: to stop you from manifesting God's glory. He lures, he deceives, he steals, attacks and destroys just to make sure he keeps us out of God's will.

Too many people have fallen victim to the oppression of the devil, too many destinies have been destroyed, too much pain and suffering has been caused. Wickedness and hatred in families, diseases that rob people of their comfort and dignity, corruption in high places, perverse criminals that destroy innocent lives, filthy and immoral conduct, demonic oppression: these are all orchestrated by the evil one.

This is the good news: the adversary, Satan, has been defeated, so you are NO LONGER a victim of his wickedness. When Jesus comes into your life, you are raised to sit in heavenly places with Christ Jesus, far above all principalities and powers. We have been made more than conquerors, through Christ Jesus. We are in a position of power, not fear.

Knowing he has just a short time before he is finally destroyed, the devil still attempts to wreak havoc and chaos in the lives of God's people; and God permits him. Yes, God is aware of the evil schemes of the devil and how he is constantly warring against the saints of God. In actual fact, the enemy can only operate because God has permitted him. Ultimately, Satan and his host of demons, along with all who work wickedness, will be destroyed; but until then God has given them the room to operate for one main reason: so that we can manifest His Glory!

The reason why God permits the devil to cause darkness, is so that you can shine your light. When the devil brings sickness, the stage is set for God's healing to flow through you; when there is chaos, you bring peace; and where there is emptiness, you manifest fruitfulness. The devil has been employed by God to set the stage for your manifestation of glory. Whenever you see evil manifesting, it should be a trigger for you to show forth God's glory.

"Now as Jesus passed by, He saw a man who was blind from birth. And His disciples asked Him, saying, 'Rabbi, who sinned, this man or his parents, that he was born blind?' Jesus answered, 'Neither this man nor his parents sinned, but that the works of God should be revealed in him.'" – John 9:1-3

Here was a man who had been blind from birth, and while the disciples were wondering what evil or sin caused this problem, Jesus saw it as an opportunity to showcase the works of God. Throughout the ministry of Jesus, He never once complained about how wicked the devil was, or worry about why people were under so much oppression. No, he just went about setting them free. What the devil meant for evil became a testimony and God was glorified. The devil has been given permission to operate, but we have also been given the authority to destroy his works. He is busy doing his job, it is about time we also get busy and do ours.

Another illustration of how God grants the devil permission is seen in the life of Job.

"Then Satan answered the LORD, 'Does Job fear God for nothing? Have you not put a hedge [of protection] around him and his house and all that he has, on every side?

You have blessed the work of his hands [and conferred prosperity and happiness upon him], and his possessions have increased in the land. But put forth Your hand now and touch (destroy) all that he has, and he will surely curse You to Your face.'

Then the LORD said to Satan, 'Behold, all that Job has is in your power, only do not put your hand on the man himself.' So Satan departed from the presence of the LORD." – Job 1:9-12 (Amplified)

When Satan went to God for permission to afflict Job, God was aware that Job will be in so much pain and suffering, but He still gave the permission because ultimately, the story of Job will be a story of glory. In one day, Job lost seven thousand sheep, three thousand camels, five hundred yoke of oxen, five hundred female donkeys, and his ten children. Later, he was afflicted with a disease that took away any form of dignity. Here was a man who was once the greatest in the East, now sitting in ashes like a pauper, covered in boils. The pain was real, and God permitted it because He knew the end.

The devil was so fixated on destroying Job that he could not see God's ultimate plan; that the end of Job would be much more than his beginning. The devil could not see that God was about to give Job double for all his trouble. The devil could not see that thousands of years after Job is gone, his story will be a source of hope and inspiration to many generations.

If God permits adversity around you, it is because it will work out a far greater weight of glory. It is like a furnace, which is characterized by great heat and pressure, and yet out of it comes great beauty and splendour. If God is the author of your story, then rest assured that the devil will not have the final say.

Kenneth Hagin was born with a deformed heart and an incurable blood disease. He became bedridden at age 15 and was expected by doctors to die at any moment. For sixteen months, this young boy was almost totally paralyzed, stuck on his bed without any hope of living a full life. That was until he decided to study the bible, beginning from the Gospel of Matthew. When he got to Mark 11:24, something was triggered inside him.

Jesus speaking in that verse, said ***"Therefore I say unto you, what things soever ye desire, when ye pray, believe that ye receive them, and ye shall have them."***

Kenneth Hagin believed the word he had just read and prayed for his healing. At that time, he did not know anyone else who believed in God's ability to heal, but he built his faith on the word and in a few days, he was out of bed for the first time in sixteen months. He began preaching from that young age and lived a fulfilled life of ministry until his death at the age of 86. His ministry was characterized by many testimonies of healing, in-depth teaching of God's word, and faith. The enemy tried to use sickness to end his life prematurely, but

God turned it around and made it the foundation for a life of impact. The one who was scheduled to die as a paralyzed teenager became an instrument of healing for many.

You may be going through some challenges right now that seem so intimidating and you cannot figure a way out. Be conscious of this truth: that challenge could not have come your way if God did not permit it. Secondly, God will only permit a challenge in your life if it will ultimately bring out the divine deposit within you.

The ultimate purpose of adversity is to reveal God's glory in your life.

CHAPTER THREE

Going Through The Furnace

*"I have refined you, but not as silver is refined.
Rather, I have refined you in the furnace of suffering."*
— Isaiah 48:10

No one appreciates the importance of a furnace as much as a goldsmith. He knows that without the furnace, he cannot bring out the beauty of the precious metal he is working on. The furnace is not comfortable, but it is necessary to bring out the fullness of beauty and glory. Gold in its raw state has potential, but is mixed with impurities that hinder its glorious manifestation. After the furnace experience, the gold comes out transformed; ready to fulfil the expectations of the goldsmith.

YOU ARE THE GOLD, GOD IS THE GOLDSMITH

Life is not a random sequence of events, nor is it a haphazard passage of time. Your life is a product of the plans, intentions and purposes of God. You are God's big idea for the fulfilment of His eternal purposes in these times. There is nothing coincidental about you. You are unique. You are God's Gold!

"For we are His workmanship, created in Christ Jesus for good works, which God prepared beforehand that we should walk in them." – Ephesians 2:10

If we are God's workmanship, then it is important to understand that, just like the goldsmith, God will take us through processes and experiences that will prepare us for His use. The furnace experience is not a punishment or a sanction for wrongdoing. It is a preparation for manifestation. The furnace represents our seasons of adversity; and in the previous chapter, we came to an understanding that the ultimate purpose of the furnace is to bring out the glory of God in our lives. How does the furnace refine us for manifestation?

REFINED UNTO OBEDIENCE

One major transformation that takes place in the furnace is our readiness to let go of our will and submit to the will of God for our lives. The impurity of disobedience is erased, and we are left with a heart that humbly says, "Yes Lord." Obedience is an essential attribute in our walk with God, without which we cannot attain the heights of glory destined for us. As we go through the furnace, we come to recognize the futility of our will, and the Sovereignty of His will.

Jonah had to spend three days in the belly of a whale to finally yield to God's will. Prior to that experience, Jonah must have been impressed with his plan to defy God's order and sail to Tarshish instead of Nineveh. The belly of the whale was not a punishment for disobedience, but a preparation for obedience. When Jonah cried out to God out of a repentant heart, God gave him another chance, and this time, Jonah was ready to obey.

The furnace of adversity provides the genuine test of obedience for the believer. Jesus, our perfect example, had to necessarily go through suffering to guarantee His obedience. In the garden of Gethsemane, burdened with grief, with his sweat like great drops of blood, knowing very well the pain and betrayal that lay ahead, Jesus came to the place of perfect obedience by saying, "Not my will, but Your will be done."

"Even though Jesus was God's Son, he learned obedience from the things he suffered. In this way, God qualified him as a perfect High Priest, and he became the source of eternal salvation for all those who obey him." – Hebrews 5:8-9 (NLT)

Obedience is not a gift; it must be learnt. Jesus went through the furnace to learn it, and so must we. The Church must come to a place of obedience to His will, even if it means going through persecution or suffering. The place of obedience is very often a place of inconvenience. If we are preoccupied with pleasing people and living in comfort, our obedience has not yet been proven. We must be refined to the point where, no matter the cost, we can also say, "Not our will, but Your will be done."

The obedience of the servants at the wedding of Cana set the tone for Jesus' first miracle. They could have refused to send the "water" to the governor of the feast, because there was no sign yet that it had become wine. They put their jobs on the line by obeying, and there was a testimony. If we want to see God's glory in our lives, obedience is compulsory; no matter the cost.

REFINED UNTO REPENTANCE

One of the great benefits of the furnace experience is that, it brings you to a place of repentance. The word repentance is derived from the Greek word metanoia, which means a change of mind, of purpose and of life. It goes beyond an emotional sense of guilt and regret; it is a shift in thinking and behaviour. God often uses the furnace of adversity to bring His people to a place where they realize their folly and repent.

Jesus told a parable of the Lost Son, (or the Prodigal Son) who wasted his father's wealth on riotous living until he came to a place of emptiness and loneliness. Prior to his suffering, he did not see anything wrong with his way of life or his decision to squander his father's wealth. He was in comfort, hence could not appreciate the need for repentance. He needed to come to the point where he envied pigs for him to realize that it was time for a change of mind and direction.

"And he would gladly have filled his stomach with the pods that the swine ate, and no one gave him anything.

But when he came to himself, he said, 'How many of my father's hired servants have bread enough and to spare, and I perish with hunger!

I will arise and go to my father, and will say to him, "Father, I have sinned against heaven and before you"'

– Luke 15:16-18

Without the furnace of affliction, it will be difficult to realize and accept that you have strayed out of God's will. It is therefore a blessing in disguise when God uses our suffering to cue us into evaluating our decisions in order to find out if we are aligned to His will. God does not delight in our pain and suffering, but He will let you go through temporary pain in order to bring you to repentance that will yield everlasting glory.

"And you shall remember that the LORD your God led you all the way these forty years in the wilderness, to humble you and test you, to know what was in your heart, whether you would keep His commandments or not.

So He humbled you, allowed you to hunger, and fed you with manna which you did not know nor did your fathers know, that He might make you know that man shall not live by bread alone; but man lives by every word that proceeds from the mouth of the LORD."

– Deuteronomy 8:2-3

The Israelites were coming from an era of slavery and heading towards the promised land. However, despite the physical change in location, they didn't have a change of mentality. They still reasoned like slaves, only interested in satisfying their basic needs of food, clothing and shelter.

God had to take them through a period of hunger to let them realize that food is not the reason for living. It was necessary for them to have a change of mindset before entering into the promised land.

It is interesting to note that just like the Israelites needed to repent before entering the promised land, the criteria for entering into the Kingdom of God is repentance. When Jesus was on earth, he began his public ministry by declaring, "Repent, for the Kingdom of God is at hand." Apostle Paul also admonishes us to be transformed *"by the renewing of your mind, that you may prove what is that good and acceptable and perfect will of God."* (Romans 12:2) So count it all joy when your Father takes you through the furnace, because your repentance will give you access to His Kingdom.

Another dimension of repentance has to do with our willingness to return to God when we step out of His will. Very often, the Israelites offended God, and He punished them by allowing other nations to oppress them or by taking them through a period of famine and lack. However, His expectation was that the punishment will bring them to a place of repentance and returning.

"Also I gave you cleanness of teeth in all your cities. And lack of bread in all your places; yet you have not returned to Me," Says the LORD.

"I also withheld rain from you, when there were still three months to the harvest. I made it rain on one city, I withheld rain from another city. One part was rained upon, and where it did not rain the part withered.

So two or three cities wandered to another city to drink water, but they were not satisfied; yet you have not returned to Me," Says the LORD.

"I blasted you with blight and mildew. When your gardens increased, your vineyards, your fig trees, and your olive trees, the locust devoured them; yet you have not returned to Me," Says the LORD.

"I sent among you a plague after the manner of Egypt; your young men I killed with a sword, along with your captive horses; I made the stench of your camps come up into your nostrils; yet you have not returned to Me," Says the LORD.

"I overthrew some of you, as God overthrew Sodom and Gomorrah, and you were like a firebrand plucked from the burning; yet you have not returned to Me," Says the LORD. – Amos 4:6-11

This was God narrating how He deliberately created hardship for His people, expecting that it would cause them to return to Him. I must state here that, Jesus has paid for every sin that has been and will be committed. Hence, God is not punishing anyone for his/her sin. Do not see adversity as a punishment from God for a wrong you did. The chastisement for your peace was laid on Jesus, so you are free from condemnation. He will use adversity, however, as a means to draw you to Himself. God did not create man to be independent, but God-dependent, and this dependency on Him must be seen at all times, especially when we encounter our seasons of adversity. When God takes us through the furnace, it is a reminder that we are designed to depend on Him, hence the need to repent and return if we have gone astray.

REFINED UNTO STRONG FAITH

"My brethren, count it all joy when you fall into various trials, knowing that the testing of your faith produces patience. But let patience have its perfect work, that you may be perfect and complete, lacking nothing." –
James 1:2-4

Count it all joy when you are going through the furnace. There is a knowledge you must have that will generate joy in your trying times; it is working out something glorious. Apostle James refers to trials as the ***"testing of your faith."*** You never know how strong your faith is until it is challenged by the storms and trials of life. The test is not meant to destroy you, but to prove how strong you are.

When a teacher prepares a class test for her students, her aim is not to make life difficult for the students. The test reveals what the students have actually learnt. Based on their response to the test, the teacher knows those who are ready to be promoted, and those who need some extra tutoring. The more tests a student passes, the more knowledgeable he/she becomes. In the school of life, your faith response to the tests of life strengthens your faith and guarantees your promotion. The test is meant to be a stepping stone, not a stumbling block.

One key attribute necessary for strong faith is patience. Another word for patience in this context is endurance: the ability to sustain your faith in spite of contrary evidence. No storm lasts forever, so it will be a shame for you to give up in the midst of the storm, when you could have endured to the end to receive your promotion. Rest assured; the storm will end.

"Weeping may endure for the night, but joy comes in the morning." – Psalms 30:5

Your "morning" will surely come; and when it does, it will surely be worth the wait. Abraham's faith in God was tested for 25 years, and at the end he was regarded as the Friend of God, and the father of faith. Your faith and patience will not be in vain.

REFINED UNTO DISTINCTION

There can be no distinction if there is no test. You cannot be crowned a champion if you have faced no opposition. The test of adversity will reveal your uniqueness and set you apart from average people. You have a purpose. You came to this world as an answer to a need of your generation. Your response when that need arises will be different from every other person, because something inside you will begin to find expression.

When Goliath and the Philistines came against Israel, the whole nation, including the very tall King Saul, had one response: fear. Well, everyone except David, a seventeen-year old boy who carried the anointing of a king. When David heard the words of Goliath, he had one focus: to bring down the uncircumcised Philistine who has dared to defy the armies of the Living God. The test of Goliath was for David's distinction.

'Then David said to the Philistine, "You come to me with a sword, with a spear, and with a javelin. But I come to you in the name of the Lord of hosts, the God of the armies of Israel, whom you have defied. This day the Lord will

deliver you into my hand, and I will strike you and take your head from you. And this day I will give the carcasses of the camp of the Philistines to the birds of the air and the wild beasts of the earth, that all the earth may know that there is a God in Israel. Then all this assembly shall know that the Lord does not save with sword and spear; for the battle is the Lord's, and He will give you into our hands."' – 1 Samuel 17:45-47

David went against Goliath with a sling and a stone, and killed the champion of the Philistines. By the end of that day, there was only one name on the lips of every Israelite: David. He was no longer in obscurity. He was the champion of Israel.

There is a champion in you waiting to find expression. See that opposition as a stepping stone designed for your next level. Just like David, you carry an anointing that empowers you for supernatural exploits.

"You are of God, little children, and have overcome them, because He who is in you is greater than he who is in the world." – 1 John 4:4

REFINED TO BE AN EXAMPLE

The best motivation to someone in distress often comes from another person who went through something similar or worse. We are more inclined to listen to those who identify with what we are going through, rather than those who just seem to know what we must do. That is why Jesus remains the perfect example for the believer. He did not just come as the only begotten Son of the Father to tell us what to do; He experienced pain, insult, betrayal, abuse, false accusations, loneliness, grief, etc. He identified with our pain and showed us how to overcome.

"Looking unto Jesus, the author and finisher of our faith, who for the joy that was set before Him endured the cross, despising the shame, and has sat down at the right hand of the throne of God.

For consider Him who endured such hostility from sinners against Himself, lest you become weary and discouraged in your souls." – Hebrews 12:2-3

In the same vein, our message to the world is best preached through our life stories. How can we testify of God's grace when we have not felt the weaknesses and inadequacies of mankind? How can we talk of His restoration power if we never lost anything? How can we reach out to our world if we are isolated from the things they go through?

Today, millions of people all over the world are blessed by the ministry of Joyce Meyer. Through her books, television programmes and conferences, she has brought healing and restoration to many people who have experienced pain, loss and abuse. Her unique ministry was birthed out of her own struggles with abuse, a failed marriage, and her quest for acceptance.

She was sexually abused by her father from a very young age; she was so depressed during her first marriage that she turned to alcohol to numb her pain; and according to her, her days had become "a living hell." But God picked her and refined her through the furnace of His word, erasing the stains of her past with the power of His love and grace. Today, she is transmitting that same love and grace to others. It has been far from a smooth journey for her, but it has all worked out for her good. Together with her husband, David, she has become a source of inspiration and hope for others facing similar struggles.

As God leads us through the furnace, He ensures that our footprints can also serve as a guide to others who may be struggling to find their way out. We become heroes and examples to others because they see us overcome the same things trying to bring them down.

As a jeweller will only display his refined products, so also will God ensure that we are refined before making us a showpiece to our world.

CHAPTER FOUR

BREAKING THE CHAINS OF IGNORANCE

"My people are destroyed for lack of knowledge..." –
Hosea 4:6a

A man's greatest enemy is his ignorance. The ignorance of
a child of God is the enemy's greatest weapon. Seasons
of adversity are meant to be temporal, and are designed to
work out God's glory. God will not permit any situation in your
life that will only end in your destruction. However, through
ignorance, a season of adversity can be extended until it
destroys the individual. God told Israel through the Prophet
Hosea that, "though you are my people, your ignorance is
destroying you." He had not stopped loving them; He still
had good thoughts and plans for them. Unfortunately, their
ignorance separated them from God's provisions and set
them on a path of destruction.

Your ignorance empowers the devil.

Satan's kingdom is referred to as the kingdom of darkness. The word translated darkness, **Skótos**, also means ignorance or error. He rules over the ignorant. In 2 Corinthians 4:4, Paul tells us Satan has blinded the minds of unbelievers so that they will not receive the light of the glorious Gospel of Christ. It is like fixing very thick curtains over your window so that the sunlight has no access to your room. He keeps the world in ignorance so that he can still reign. He has no power over those who know their God. Every child of God has been placed far above the power of the devil, for we are seated in heavenly places in Christ Jesus (Ephesians 4:6). However, through ignorance, a believer can cede his place of authority and be tormented by the devil. When the devil came to tempt Jesus in the wilderness, as recorded in Luke 4, he was just looking out for a loophole of ignorance in order to pounce. But Jesus knew his stuff!

If the enemy will keep a believer poor, it is because that believer is ignorant about God's provision for prosperity. If a believer remains oppressed by sickness, then knowledge about God's provision for our health is lacking. As long as we remain ignorant, we give the enemy the right to keep us in bondage.

GOD'S WORD IS LIGHT

Darkness only prevails because light is absent. As soon as light is introduced, there is no need for a debate or an argument; darkness leaves. Just as darkness represents ignorance, light represents knowledge. The Psalmist declares that the entrance of God's Word into a person gives light (Psalm 119:30). An encounter with the light of the Word brings an end to every oppression of darkness.

"And you shall know the truth, and the truth shall make you free." – John 8:32

We must understand that there is no deliverance or help that God will give a man that will not be derived from the Word. The Word of God is the delivery system of the Kingdom, and those who encounter the light (knowledge) contained in the Word can never be oppressed by darkness.

"He sent His word and healed them, and delivered them from their destructions." – Psalm 107:20

Whenever God is bringing an end to a season of adversity, what He sends is a word. If that word is received in a heart of faith and applied to a situation, it produces light that will end every darkness. The right application of this knowledge derived from the Word is called wisdom. In Matthew 7:24, Jesus said, whoever structures his life based on the Word is like a wise man who built on the rock. No matter the season of adversity that comes, that house (life) will still be standing strong.

WISDOM IS THE PRINCIPAL THING

"Wisdom is the principal thing; therefore get wisdom. And in all your getting, get understanding." – Proverbs 4:7

The word "principal" means the first in place, time, order or rank. The first thing you must have is wisdom; light derived from God's Word. In Genesis 1, when God met a dark and chaotic world, the first thing He created was light. God did not create in darkness. In the same vein, if you want a turnaround in any situation, light/wisdom must be your principal thing. Our prayers and every other thing we do in our walk with God will only be beneficial in an environment of wisdom. In Matthew 25, we have a story of 10 virgins who had the privilege of meeting the bridegroom, who is Christ. It is important to note that five of those virgins missed out on that opportunity of a lifetime because they were foolish; their lives were not founded on wisdom. Being born-again without wisdom makes you a foolish virgin; you miss out on the benefits of the Kingdom. There is no substitute for wisdom in God's Kingdom. It establishes your dominion and guarantees your victory.

"For I will give you a mouth and wisdom, which all your adversaries will not be able to contradict or resist." – Luke 21:15

IT TAKES GODLY WISDOM TO REIGN

The Bible clearly differentiates between the wisdom of men and the wisdom of God. The wisdom of men makes you operate as a natural man on the earth, analysing and reasoning according to your physical senses. It is the wisdom available to fallen man to enable him excel on the earth. It can be acquired through our educational systems, reading and studying the works of men, interacting with wise men in order to be wise, etc. This wisdom however, cannot cause a man to reign as God intended him to. It is limited and cannot understand the will and purposes of God. To walk in God's will, we need a higher wisdom.

"However, we speak wisdom among those who are mature, yet not the wisdom of this age, nor of the rulers of this age, who are coming to nothing.

But we speak the wisdom of God in a mystery, the hidden wisdom which God ordained before the ages for our glory." – 1 Corinthians 2:6,7

The wisdom that guarantees our victory is not characterized by academic degrees, social status or public opinion. It is not wisdom that a man can give, because it is hidden to the natural man. God hid it from the world, and kept it exclusively for the church! This wisdom is received by revelation; it has to be unveiled to a man by the Holy Spirit.

The Holy Spirit is the one mandated to lead us into the truth and wisdom that sets free and establishes dominion. No matter how much effort a man puts in to acquire this wisdom, it will be an exercise in futility without the Spirit of God.

"However, when He, the Spirit of Truth, has come, He will guide you into all truth; for He will not speak on His own authority, but whatever He hears He will speak; and He will tell you things to come." – John 16:13

Our access to the wisdom of God is the Spirit of God; there is no other way. He searches the deep things of God and reveals it to us. Every child of God can receive the Holy Spirit, and anyone who receives Him has access to all truth. Paul told the church at Corinth that the wisdom was hidden for our glory (1 Corinthians 2:7). It means our glory is hinged on our ability to receive the revelation of this wisdom. What a joy to know that the Holy Spirit is always ready and eager to grant us access to this wisdom.

REVELATION BRINGS ELEVATION

"And Pharaoh said to his servants, 'Can we find such a one as this, a man in whom is the Spirit of God?'

Then Pharaoh said to Joseph, 'Inasmuch as God has shown you all this, there is no one as discerning and wise as you.

You shall be over my house, and all my people shall be ruled according to your word; only in regard to the throne will I be greater than you.'" – Genesis 41:38-40

Revelation of divine wisdom was the key that turned a prisoner to a prime minister in a day. The answer to Pharaoh's dream was hidden by God for the lifting and promotion of Joseph. It was so divine that, the gentile king of Egypt could testify that the Spirit of God was in Joseph.

Daniel had a similar experience in Babylon, moving from just being one of the wise men, to become the ruler of the whole province of Babylon and the chief of the governors. (Daniel 2:48)

We are living in times where the world is looking for so many answers. God's people must realize that there are solutions that have been hidden for our glory. Through revelation, we can rise to a place of prominence and be the light of the world.

Just like Jacob was given a divine secret for success in his agricultural business, you too can access divine secrets for a financial turnaround. A woman who was so indebted that her two sons were about to be taken, received a revelation of divine wisdom that launched her into financial independence. (2 Kings 4:1-7)

The Spirit of God is still revealing secrets today!

"If any of you lacks wisdom, let him ask of God, who gives to all liberally and without reproach, and it will be given to him." *– James 1:5*

There are secrets and truths that have been hidden in ages past, waiting for us to come, because they were ordained for our glory. There is a certain dimension of wisdom that will cause us to reign on earth; it is that wisdom that will make us live as the light of the world and the salt of the earth. Not only is that wisdom available, but we also carry within us, the Spirit of God who is mandated to lead us into these hidden truths. All we need to do is **ASK**, because God gives liberally.

STRENGTH IN YOUR INNER MAN

"If you faint in the day of adversity, your strength is small." – Proverbs 24:10

You must be strong in order to overcome. This is not physical strength, but the strength that comes from the Holy Spirit within you. Your physical strength or abilities will be of no use if you are not strong within. When David went up to meet Goliath, he was not the strongest Israelite, physically speaking. But within him, he carried the invincible strength of God.

"May He (God) grant you out of the riches of His glory, to be strengthened and spiritually energized with power through His Spirit in your inner self, [indwelling your innermost being and personality]." – Ephesians 3:16 (Amplified)

The Holy Spirit within us is not an idle passenger. He supplies us with strength in our inner man. Jesus was above every challenge of life because He had the anointing (empowerment) of the Holy Spirit.

"The Spirit of the Lord is upon Me, because He has anointed Me to preach the gospel to the poor; He has sent

Me to heal the brokenhearted, to proclaim liberty to the captives and recovery of sight to the blind, to set at liberty those who are oppressed; to proclaim the acceptable year of the Lord." – Luke 4:18-19.

"How God anointed Jesus of Nazareth with the Holy Spirit and with power, who went about doing good and healing all who were oppressed by the devil, for God was with Him." – Acts 10:38

Jesus healed the sick, silenced storms, walked on water, cast out devils, because He was anointed with the Holy Spirit and power. The Holy Spirit within you grants you access to power that can change lives and transform situations. The empowerment of the Holy Spirit is the anointing that breaks every yoke. If situations of life could not keep Jesus down, then they cannot keep you down because you are also anointed with the Holy Spirit.

WHERE ARE YOU?

No matter how much you desire to reach a particular destination, your chances of getting there are close to nil if you cannot accurately determine your current position. Even the most sophisticated navigational systems will find it impossible to give you directions if they cannot first determine where you are currently. One of the major reasons why people struggle to step out of the maze of adversity is their inability to identify where they are.

It is not a matter of geography but rather an ability to honestly analyse your current situation in relation to your purpose, abilities and expected destination. Imagine a driver whose vehicle is stuck in mud, but is still comfortable sitting behind the steering wheel. The car seat still feels comfortable, the stereo is still playing his favourite song, the air condition seems to be working just fine, and so he does not see that he has a problem. He has cushioned himself with a false reality that blinds him from realizing that he is stuck. A tow truck will pass by and he won't bother to ask for help.

Where am I? What is my current location on this journey of life, and how long have I been at this spot? It is not a time to play the blame game and point fingers at others. It is the point where you tell yourself, ***"This is my life, and it is my responsibility to make it work."***

Jesus met a man who was blind and asked him, ***"What can I do for you?"*** (Mark 10:51) Our ability to receive the help of God in a situation is determined by our ability to recognize that we need His help in that particular area. If you do not acknowledge that you are having financial struggles, you will not seek for God's wisdom concerning prosperity, and that problem will not go away. You can pretend to have a happy marriage in front of the world, but pretending is not a solution to your problem. God can give you wisdom for that marriage if only you will acknowledge your need for it.

You can only receive the help you ask for. Remember, God will always give grace to the humble. Be humble enough to ask for His help, and He will grant you the wisdom and the strength you need.

CHAPTER FIVE

Declare Your Victory

Your silence is the enemy's license.

"By faith we understand that the worlds were framed by the word of God, so that the things which are seen were not made of things which are visible." – Hebrews 11:3

We have already seen that God encountered a negative situation on earth and He turned it around. One key phrase we see as God deals with a chaotic earth is, *"And God said, . . ."* Everything exists because He spoke.

Through His Word, God framed chaos into beauty, emptiness into abundance, and darkness into light. Nothing happened until He began to speak. Let me remind you that you have been created in His image.

Your victory is waiting for your declaration to find expression in your life. As a child of God, your words are not just for communication and expression, but they are for creation. There are things that will remain in the unseen realm until you speak.

DO NOT SPEAK ABOUT THE PROBLEM, SPEAK TO IT!

"For assuredly, I say to you, whoever says to this mountain, 'Be removed and be cast into the sea,' and does not doubt in his heart, but believes that those things he says will be done, he will have whatever he says." – Mark 11:23

Faith is powerful; it can move mountains, calm seas and even make the sun stand still. But the power of faith is only made manifest when we speak. Your words are an indication of the contents of your heart. If your heart is full of faith, you will speak faith. If your heart is full of fear, you will speak fear.

You cannot afford to be silent over the issues of your life, because your silence permits the enemy to take over. Your mouth is a weapon against the enemy, and how you use it will determine your victory or misery.

"For I will give you a mouth and wisdom which all your adversaries will not be able to contradict or resist." – Luke 21:15

Your mouth is not meant for complaining; it is not meant for you to describe your problems or exaggerate your pain. God has given you a mouth to declare victory that the enemy cannot resist.

You have the responsibility to declare God's word over your life. Declare joy, even when you feel depressed; declare God's abundance in the face of emptiness; call forth your children by faith, even when you are described as barren. Frame your world with your words and bring an end to every negative situation.

"For by your words you will be justified, and by your words you will be condemned." – Matthew 12:37

CREATE THE RIGHT ENVIRONMENT

Very often, our words are conditioned by the environment we find ourselves in. It will be very difficult to declare victory over your life when you are surrounded by pessimists and negative-thinkers. If you listen to people who mock God's word they will water down your faith.

Jesus was on his way to heal the daughter of Jairus when word came that she was now dead. Prior to this time, there was a crowd following him on his way there, but when he heard that the situation had gotten worse, he sent them all away and only went to the house with Peter, James, and John. (Mark 5:37) He selected those who should be around him because he needed the right environment.

Not everyone must be around you when you are going through a season of adversity. Not everyone must hear your story while you are on your way to victory. Be deliberate about the environment you create around you.

When Jesus got to Jairus' house, there was another negative environment he had to deal with.

"Then He came to the house of the ruler of the synagogue, and saw a tumult and those who wept and wailed loudly.

When He came in, He said to them, "Why make this commotion and weep? The child is not dead, but sleeping."

And they ridiculed Him. But when He had put them all outside, He took the father and the mother of the child, and those who were with Him, and entered where the child was lying.

Then He took the child by the hand, and said to her, "Talitha, cumi," which is translated, "Little girl, I say to you, arise."

Immediately the girl arose and walked, for she was twelve years of age. And they were overcome with great amazement." – Mark 5:38-42

If Jesus needed the right environment for victory, then so do you. You might have to spend less time with certain people, avoid certain conversations and keep yourself from gatherings that will water down your faith. Spend more time with people who will boost your faith and trust in God.

It is what you feed your spirit that responds in time of adversity. If you feed your spirit with the Word of God through study and meditation, it builds in you a reservoir of faith that equips you to respond to any situation of life. Joshua was told to meditate and obey the commandments of God if he wanted good success. (Joshua 1:8) That is true for us too.

THE NAME OF JESUS

"Therefore God also has highly exalted Him and given Him the name which is above every name, that at the

Everything is subject to the authority in the name of Jesus; in heaven, on earth, and under the earth. If that challenge is within these three spheres, then it has no choice than to bow to the name of Jesus. The name of Jesus gives authority to every believer to effect change on earth and subject every situation to the will of God. Sickness and disease, poverty, depression, failure, addictions, barrenness, demonic oppressions; all these can be brought to an end by the power in the name of Jesus.

In the third chapter of the Book of Acts, there is a story of a man who was born lame and had decided to use his disability as a leverage to court sympathy by begging at the temple. Every day, he was carried to the temple and laid at the gate called Beautiful begging worshippers as they entered. One day, as Peter and John were entering the temple, he asked them for alms.

"Then Peter said, "Silver and gold I do not have, but what I do have I give you: in the name of Jesus Christ of Nazareth, rise up and walk." And he took him by the right hand and lifted him up, and immediately his feet

and ankle bones received strength. So he, leaping up, stood and walked and entered the temple with them – walking, leaping and praising God." – Acts 3:6-8

Years of adversity were wiped away in a moment through the power in the name of Jesus. The man had been searching for the wrong things all his life; the sympathy of men and their money. But it took something superior to bring an end to his suffering: the name of Jesus.

The next day, the high priest, elders and scribes at Jerusalem summoned Peter and John to ask them one question: ***"By what power or by what name have you done this?"*** (Acts 4:7) Who gave you the audacity to end this man's suffering and give him a new life?

Friend, it takes power and authority to end cycles of adversity and bondage. The expression of God's glory in your life must be backed by an authority. Jesus is that authority.

"And Jesus came and spoke to them, saying, 'All authority has been given to Me in heaven and on earth.'"
– Matthew 28:18

"If you ask anything in my name, I will do it." – John 14:14

When we speak and declare in His name, we are not being religious; we are invoking power and authority that causes change. When we call the name Jesus, the devil and his agents flee. When we pray in His name, all things are possible. We do not beg our way to the top; we declare it by faith, because the one with all power and authority lives in us. Declare your victory in the name of Jesus!

THE SUPERNATURAL ENVIRONMENT OF PRAISE

When we praise, all things are possible because praise creates an environment for God to showcase His strength in the lives of His people.

"Who is like You, O Lord, among the gods? Who is like You, glorious in holiness, fearful in praises, doing wonders?" – Exodus 15:11

Our God is fearful in praises. When we praise, we are effectively saying, "God, it's time for you to show up and show off." When we praise, the enemy gets scared because we magnify God's strength in our lives and invoke supernatural victory. When we praise, we get God to be personally involved in the situation.

One of the most amazing testimonies of victory through praise is recorded in 2 Chronicles 20. Three nations gathered together to wage war against Judah. Jehoshaphat, the king of Judah knew very well that his army could not handle the military might of these three nations, so he turned to the One who is greater than all armies of the world put together. This was the response God gave through Prophet Jahaziel.

"You will not need to fight in this battle. Position yourselves, stand still and see the salvation of the Lord, who is with you, O Judah and Jerusalem! Do not fear or be dismayed; tomorrow go out against them, for the Lord is with you." – 2 Chronicles 20:17

When you create an environment of praise, your weaknesses and inadequacies become irrelevant because God takes over. You just need to "Position Yourself." Jehoshaphat's response to God's word was to worship and praise God, together with all the inhabitants of Judah. The next morning, as they were about to go to war, Jehoshaphat appointed singers who would praise the **"Beauty of Holiness"**, while the army follows behind. Who goes to war with singers in front of the army? Obviously, someone who is ready to see the Mighty Hand of God at work.

Judah did not have to lift a finger to fight. God set the three nations against each other and they destroyed themselves. When Judah got there, there were dead bodies all over; none escaped.

Dear friend, you cannot afford to fight the battles of life with your own strength. It will be too costly. But if you can create an environment of praise, God will fight for you; for indeed, He inhabits (dwells in) the praise of His people. He does not dwell in complaining or murmuring. He does not dwell in tears of pain and suffering. Your praise is your God-environment.

We could talk about Paul and Silas who were locked up and chained in prison for preaching the gospel. Instead of feeling sad and discouraged, they praised God! And as they gave God praise in that prison, the chains fell off and the prison doors were opened without any human effort. Their praise brought the presence of God into the prison. When God is around, no chains can hold you down!

Praise God for your deliverance! Praise Him for your healing! Praise Him for your prosperity! Praise Him for your all-round victory!

Your life will not remain the same.

CHAPTER SIX

Don't Give Up

Faith, which is the guarantee of our victory, is persistent; it never gives up. Faith is steadfast and unshaking because it is not based on situations or emotions, but on the Word of God which does not change, but abides forever. If what is happening in your life is not consistent with what God has spoken about you, then don't accept it as permanent. It will change.

The only thing that will abide forever is God's Word. Anything that is not a product of God's word is temporary. If you hold on to God's Word by faith, there will be a change. Failure is not permanent, because it is not in God's will for you. Sickness is illegal because by the stripes of Jesus, we are healed. Barrenness cannot dwell with you, because God blessed you and commanded you to be fruitful and multiply.

You may be going through a phase that seems contrary to what God has spoken over you. You may be like a Joseph who has dreams of being a ruler but finds himself as a slave and a prisoner in a foreign land. You may be like a David who has been anointed King of Israel, but is living in caves and hiding from Saul. You may be like an Abraham, who has a promise of God to be a father of many nations, but still has no child. Just like all these examples, that seemingly negative phase will come to pass. It is just a precursor to the manifestation of your victory.

LIFE'S OBSTACLES, GOD'S MIRACLES

When the wine ran out at the wedding feast, Mary knew there was only one person who could fix it; Jesus. It was clear that there was no other way they could have gotten another supply of wine to salvage the feast, so she refused to be discouraged by Jesus' initial reluctance to get involved. She needed a miracle and she was not about to give up on the Miracle-worker.

Just like Mary, we also encounter obstacles on the journey of life that require miracles. No matter how well we plan and strategize, life has a way of catching us off-guard and very often we are faced with battles that we cannot win on our own. Be it a natural disaster, a health challenge, a failing business, an unfaithful spouse, a wayward child; people are fighting battles that they are not equipped to handle.

I am writing this book at a time when the world is dealing with the coronavirus pandemic and almost every aspect of human life has been affected; churches in most countries have had to suspend their gatherings in church buildings and rely on online services, schools all over the world have been closed down, people have lost their jobs, economies of the world have taken a big hit, and most tragically, thousands of lives have been lost. Every now and then, life reminds us that it can be unpredictable in a terrifying way. However, no matter what life throws at us, God always has an answer. And sometimes, the answer goes beyond our human reasoning.

GOD IS A MIRACLE-WORKER

A miracle is God's supernatural intervention in the natural affairs of men. It is Divine strength overshadowing humanity's weakness to guarantee victory on earth. A miracle is beyond human ability or reasoning; science cannot explain it and nature cannot reproduce it. A miracle is God at work in the lives of His children.

"You are the God of great wonders! You demonstrate your awesome power among the nations."* – Psalm 77:14 (NLT)*

There is no scientific explanation to how water from a pot can turn to wine, or how a sea can be parted for people to walk through it on dry ground, or how five loaves of bread and two fish can feed five thousand men plus women and children. Sicknesses flee, barrenness is destroyed, demons are cast out, yokes are broken, lives are transformed, all by the power of God. Whenever God steps into a situation, miracles become evident because He is Supernatural; miracles reflect His nature. Therefore, if God is with you, you should expect miracles in your life.

BE EXPECTANT

Expectation is the womb that ushers miracles into the lives of God's people. Faith is essentially an expectation that is birthed from confidence in the integrity and ability of God. Several times, Jesus would attribute a miracle he performed to the faith of the recipient. Even when he was not conscious of it, like in the case of the woman with the issue of blood, the expectation was great enough to pull virtue out of Him. If you do not have a desire to see the supernatural power of God at work in your life, rest assured nothing supernatural would come your way. But if you can have a level of hunger and desire for God's miracle-working power, He will do exceeding abundantly above all you can ever ask or think.

GOD CHANGES TIMES AND SEASONS

"Blessed be the name of God forever and ever, for wisdom and might are His.

And He changes the times and the seasons; He removes kings and raises up kings; He gives wisdom to the wise and knowledge to those who have understanding." – Daniel 2:20-21

Everything that happens on earth is regulated by time. God dwells in eternity but instituted time to regulate affairs on earth. A season is simply a period of time with a distinct characteristic or feature. We can have rainy season, because it is a period of time where there is regular rainfall. In temperate regions of the world, there is a season known as winter which has snow as its distinct feature.

Seasons are subject to change. Winter will give way to Spring, the rainy season will give way to Harmattan. No season of life is permanent. Even our good and pleasant seasons of life must be upgraded to better seasons. You cannot remain at the same level.

The good news is that God has the power to change times and seasons. God has the ability to bring an end to every season of adversity in your life, and He does not need anyone's permission to do that. Daniel declared that when God changes seasons, He sets up kings and brings down kings. In effect, He brings every situation into conformity to His will.

When God changed Hannah's season, she was no longer the barren and bitter wife of Elkanah, but the proud mother of Samuel, one of Israel's greatest prophets. In praise, she declared:

"The Lord makes poor and makes rich; He brings low and lifts up.

He raises the poor from the dust and lifts the beggar from the ash heap, to set them among princes and make them inherit the throne of glory. For the pillars of the earth are the Lord's, and He has set the world upon them." – 1 Samuel 2:7-8.

God is responsible for your change of season, so keep your eyes fixed on Him, and don't lose faith. One of the reasons why Abraham is considered the father of faith is because for 25 years, he held on to a promise even when there was no physical sign that God will come through.

"He did not waver at the promise of God through unbelief, but was strengthened in faith, giving glory to God." – Romans 4:20

If you have received a promise of God, do not waver. Stand firm in your faith, no matter how long it takes, because God is always faithful. You are who God says you are. Your circumstances do not have the power to define you or determine what you can be unless you permit them. You are blessed, regardless of the bills staring at you. You are fruitful, not barren. You are healed because God says so.

No one encounters glory by giving up. There is no reward for quitters. No one who is double-minded can receive God's victory.

"But let him ask in faith, with no doubting, for he who doubts is like a wave of the sea driven and tossed by the wind.

For let not that man suppose that he will receive anything from the Lord." – James 1:6-7

GOD REWARDS PERSISTENCE

Jesus gave a parable in Luke 18 of a widow who went to an unjust judge seeking vengeance against her adversary. The judge did not fear God nor regard men, so he had no intention of helping the widow. However, the widow kept coming to him for help until he finally succumbed to her pressure. Jesus said:

"And shall God not avenge His own elect who cry out day and night to Him, though He bears long with them?

I tell you that He will avenge them speedily. Nevertheless, when the Son of Man comes, will He really find faith on the earth?"

– Luke 18:7-8

The widow kept coming to the unjust judge because she was convinced without a doubt that he had what it took to help her. When we are persistent in seeking the help of God, we are effectively saying that we acknowledge His ability to help us and change our situations. Persistence is a proof of trust and confidence in the character and ability of God. Persistence says, "God, I know you can do it, so I will keep praying and I will keep praising until my change comes." Persistence is faith in action, and without faith it is impossible to please God.

You may have sought the help of God concerning an issue and might not have received an answer yet. Do not give up, and do not grow weary. Keep asking, keep seeking, and keep knocking. Your victory will surely come.

CHAPTER SEVEN

YOU ARE LOVED BY GOD

"The Lord has appeared of old to me, saying: 'Yes, I have loved you with an everlasting love; therefore with lovingkindness I have drawn you.'" – Jeremiah 31:3

God's love for us is the foundation of our relationship with Him. It is everlasting; we cannot trace its beginning nor find its end. Because of that love, while we were yet sinners, Christ paid the price for our redemption and gave us the right to become God's children. His love is not a reaction to our good deeds or pious lifestyle, because it preceded our very existence. His love cannot be extinguished by our mistakes, errors and attitudes because that Divine Love has paid the price for every sin and borne the consequences for every mistake. Prophet Isaiah said, ". . . the chastisement (punishment required) for our peace was upon Him." (Isaiah 53:5) His love cannot be manipulated or corrupted because He does not have love, HE IS Love.

If you are loved by God, then you must realize that you are not going through a difficult period because God is angry and wants to punish you. Your trials are not meant to appease God for your mistakes. Jesus already took care of all that on the cross for you.

Yes, there's an accuser of the saints who will always make you feel like you are being punished for something you did, or make you feel you do not deserve God's mercy and help because you are not worthy. He uses the weapon of guilt to keep you away from receiving the help of God. But you must know that the accuser is the father of lies. You deserve God's mercy and help because Jesus has made you worthy. If you are born-again, then you are now a member of God's family and your Father loves you too much to see you perish.

COME BOLDLY

"Let us therefore come boldly to the throne of grace, that we may obtain mercy and find grace to help in time of need." - Hebrews 4:16

We must come to God boldly; with confidence and without

fear. If earthly fathers with limited love can feel obligated to come to the aid of their children, how much more your heavenly Father who is the epitome of love and mercy.

When we come to God boldly, we position ourselves to receive an appropriate blessing at the right moment. We encounter His grace which empowers us to overcome every situation of life. There is a blessing of abundance for every moment of lack. There is a blessing of strength for every moment of weakness. There is a blessing of wisdom and peace for every moment of confusion. There is a blessing of fruitfulness for every moment of barrenness.

There is no situation of life that the Love of God has not already provided a solution to. There is no error that His Love has not already corrected. There is no hurt or pain that His Love cannot heal.

"For His divine power has bestowed on us [absolutely] everything necessary for [a dynamic spiritual] life and godliness, through true and personal knowledge of Him who called us by His own glory and excellence." – 2 Peter 1:3 (Amplified)

One major reason why we must come boldly is because God has called us by His glory and excellence. You have been made a partaker of His divine nature, and so your life is His business. Your victory brings Him glory. He has made you the evidence of His glory to your generation. He cannot therefore sit idly while seasons of adversity knock you out.

If only we could know how much He loves us, we would have no fear. If only we could realize the depth of His love for us, we would know that all things are working together for our good, because we are called according to His purpose. If only we could see the glorious height of His love for us, we would realize that even in our troubles, He is right there with us; strengthening us and leading us out into glory.

"When you pass through the waters, I will be with you; and through the rivers, they shall not overflow you. When you walk through the fire, you shall not be burned, nor shall the flame scorch you."

– Isaiah 43:2

No matter what you are going through, you are not alone. He has promised never to leave nor forsake you; and He will not fail. That season of adversity is working out God's glory in your life.

HE LIVES IN YOU

"You are of God, little children, and have overcome them, because He who is in you is greater than he who is in the world." - 1 John 4:4

So great is the Father's love for us that He has placed His Holy Spirit within us. We are carriers of God's divine presence. No obstacle of life can withstand the presence of God. No demon in hell can keep you bound when you carry the presence of God.

You may be going through fire right now, but God says you will not be burned. This means, that situation will not be the definition of your life. You may be passing through turbulent waters, but He will not allow you to drown. He is with you and will give you the grace to walk on those waters.

You are not a victim. You are God's Beloved. You are an expression of His glory and a testimony of His grace. Your victory is certain and your destiny is secure in God, in Jesus' name! Amen!

ELORM MENSA MINISTRIES INTERNATIONAL
ACCRA - GHANA

www.elormmensa.com
Tel: +233 209 304007